Praise for *Beyond Blame*

Learning from the past is incredibly difficult, despite what our hindsight-colored glasses might lead us to believe. Zwieback tells a tale that is all too familiar to many, and does an excellent job introducing the reader to the new perspective on errors, mistakes, and accidents. This perspective sits upon a firm foundation of scientific research across many disciplines over decades, and Dave presents it quite nicely.

—John Allspaw, CTO at Etsy

Beyond Blame reminds the reader to assess difficult situations from multiple, diverse viewpoints, consciously addressing the individual biases that play a much larger role in our lives than we would expect. The easily recognisable everyday situations portrayed in the book illustrate the destructive nature of blameful environments, their effect on both the organisations and individuals, and ways to overcome them.

—Kaimar Karu, Head of ITSM at AXELOS

Dave Zwieback has a knack for telling stories that show how to take an organization from a culture of blame, fear, and distrust to one that enables real accountability and learning. An insightful, practical, and indispensable read for any executive wishing to effectively manage complex systems and organizations.

—Pedro Canahuati, Director, Production Engineering and Site Reliability at Facebook

This is a highly practical and accessible guide to critical, and possibly counter-intuitive, rules of the road in working with complex system breakdowns, guidelines that are increasingly essential as our world becomes ever more wired together.

—*Michael Chender, Founding Chair of ALIA (formerly Shambhala Institute for Authentic Leadership) and founder and CEO of Metals Economics Group*

Beyond Blame beautifully illustrates why and how organizations benefit from putting trust in their teams and adopting more just and human-centered cultures.

—*Mathias Meyer, CEO at Travis CI*

Dave Zwieback's tale masterfully dissects the gross and the subtle ways in which blame undermines functional and productive behaviours in our workplaces and in our personal lives: A must-read to cut through all clutter created by shying away from taking responsibility for what we do and who we are.

—*Dr. Anja Hartmann, Executive Counsellor, Owner and Principal at bucketrider.org*

In this parable about IT's well-intentioned but vicious cycle of incident responses, Dave Zwieback has given us a great gift: the ability to see the dynamics in our organizations more clearly. He gently, yet convincingly, helps us understand how our intuitive reactions work against us, because our prior experiences create biases and assumptions that reinforce the systems that sabotaged us in the first place. More importantly, as the title suggests, he shows how we and our teams can respond more empathetically, and build more intelligent and resilient organizations.

—*Baron Schwartz, CEO at VividCortex*

Finally a book for non-technical managers and executives that explains what really causes outages and how they can create a culture that prevents outages by learning from them. This book will change your life, and your company!

—*Thomas A. Limoncelli, co-author of*
The Practice of Cloud System Administration

Beyond Blame

Learning from Failure and Success

Dave Zwieback

Beijing · Boston · Farnham · Sebastopol · Tokyo

Beyond Blame: Learning from Failure and Success

by Dave Zwieback

Printed in the United States of America.

Published by O'Reilly Media, Inc., 1005 Gravenstein Highway North, Sebastopol, CA 95472.

O'Reilly books may be purchased for educational, business, or sales promotional use. Online editions are also available for most titles (*http://safaribooksonline.com*). For more information, contact our corporate/institutional sales department: 800-998-9938 or *corporate@oreilly.com*.

Editors: Courtney Nash and Brian Anderson	**Interior Designer:** Monica Kamsvaag
Production Editor: Nicole Shelby	**Cover Designers:** Edie Freeman and Ellie Volck-hausen
Copyeditor: Jasmine Kwityn	
Proofreader: Sharon Wilkey	**Illustrator:** Rebecca Demarest
Indexer: WordCo Indexing Services	

October 2015:   First Edition

Revision History for the First Edition

2015-10-06:   First Release
2016-04-01:   Second Release

See *http://oreilly.com/catalog/errata.csp?isbn=9781491906415* for release details.

978-1-491-90641-5

[LSI]

*For the son of a poet, painter of light, without whom I still would not know
I am a wanderer*

Contents

Preface

Our increasingly complex world demands that we continuously learn in order to survive and thrive. Luckily, it offers us endless opportunities to learn from failures and successes, big and small, at work and at home. This short book is a mirror that helps us recognize when instead of learning we are too quick to blame, punish, judge, oversimplify.

This book is grounded in theories of complexity science, resilience engineering, human factors, cognitive science, and organizational psychology. It is also based on what the attendees of the Awesome Postmortems workshops (which Yulia Sheynkman and I created and have been conducting since early 2014) have taught us about the practice of learning from failure and success.

While the incident in the book is fictional, it should be all too familiar to anyone who works with (and in) complex systems. In an instinctive rush toward closure, we jump to conclusions, and construct simplistic stories of what happened and who's to blame (or to praise). Comfortable as these stories might be, they short-circuit our learning. Only by going beyond blame—and by working together to overcome bias—can we construct more realistic and helpful narratives that allow us to learn more fully. Going beyond blame enables us to make our systems more resilient, and build more just and humane learning organizations.

Safari® Books Online

 *Safari Books Online* is an on-demand digital library that delivers expert *content* in both book and video form from the world's leading authors in technology and business.

Technology professionals, software developers, web designers, and business and creative professionals use Safari Books Online as their primary resource for research, problem solving, learning, and certification training.

Safari Books Online offers a range of plans and pricing for enterprise, government, education, and individuals.

Members have access to thousands of books, training videos, and prepublication manuscripts in one fully searchable database from publishers like O'Reilly Media, Prentice Hall Professional, Addison-Wesley Professional, Microsoft Press, Sams, Que, Peachpit Press, Focal Press, Cisco Press, John Wiley & Sons, Syngress, Morgan Kaufmann, IBM Redbooks, Packt, Adobe Press, FT Press, Apress, Manning, New Riders, McGraw-Hill, Jones & Bartlett, Course Technology, and hundreds more. For more information about Safari Books Online, please visit us online.

How to Contact Us

Please address comments and questions concerning this book to the publisher:

> O'Reilly Media, Inc.
> 1005 Gravenstein Highway North
> Sebastopol, CA 95472
> 800-998-9938 (in the United States or Canada)
> 707-829-0515 (international or local)
> 707-829-0104 (fax)

We have a web page for this book, where we list errata, examples, and any additional information. You can access this page at *http://bit.ly/beyond-blame*.

To comment or ask technical questions about this book, send email to *book-questions@oreilly.com*.

For more information about our books, courses, conferences, and news, see our website at *http://www.oreilly.com*.

Find us on Facebook: *http://facebook.com/oreilly*

Follow us on Twitter: *http://twitter.com/oreillymedia*

Watch us on YouTube: *http://www.youtube.com/oreillymedia*

Acknowledgments

I am deeply grateful to everyone who contributed time, energy, knowledge, and ideas to this book, especially John Allspaw, Brian Anderson, Kevin Behr, Benjamin Chait, Michael Chender, Brad Cottel, Jennelle Crothers, Patrick Debois, Sidney Dekker, Jessica DeVita, Oren Ellenbogen, Rolan Gregg, JD Harrington, Anja Hartmann, Jon Jensen, Robb Kidd, Gene Kim, Kristian Kristensen, Tom Limoncelli, Dave Mangot, Mathias Meyer, Zoran Perkov, Phil Sarin, Baron Schwartz, David Snowden, Jeff Sussna, James Turnbull, and David Woods. That the book is even readable is due to the extensive surgery it received from Trish Deitch.

I wrote in short bursts from the fall of 2014 to the fall of 2015 in between long periods of laziness and panic. A big part was written during a March 2015 "hack week" at Next Big Sound, whose cofounders (Alex White, David Hoffman, and Samir Rayani) created the best place I've ever worked.

This book could not exist without Yulia's constant encouragement and love. May the following pages make the world a little better for Zack and Ati, and help their generation go fearlessly beyond blame.

Executive Action

"This can't happen again," Roger said, looking directly at Bill, his gaze piercing, almost brutal. They were sitting across from each other at a massive wooden table polished to perfection. Despite his restrained demeanor, Roger, the son of a British diplomat, was furious. Even sitting down, he towered over everyone in the room. Roger had a thin face and a full head of white hair. In his fitted, dark-blue suit, pink shirt, and gold cufflinks, he was the only formally dressed person in the room. Roger's other direct reports—heads of all the I.T. groups at the firm where Roger was chief information officer—were seated around the table.

"Just last week," he said, "I had to explain to the Executive Committee the reasons for the previous outage."

"I take full responsibility for this one," Bill said, trying not to look away.

As if he hadn't heard, Roger continued. "I had to stand there like an amateur and assure them that we have the expertise to keep the firm's infrastructure running smoothly. And now the network is down on the day we have the highest volume of trades on record?"

Roger finally acknowledged Bill. "Do you have an explanation?"

Bill sighed. He was short, slightly overweight, with what little remained of his blond hair closely cropped. He wore rimless glasses and his blue polo shirt untucked. His beige khakis were held up by a brown leather belt, sagging under the weight of two smartphones in black holsters.

He was the head of the firm's networking group, which operated one of the largest telecommunications networks in the world—a fact not widely known outside the insular world of financial institutions. The network tied together all the firm's offices, and connected it to all its partners and markets around the globe.

"We run a pretty large network," Bill said. "And it's been engineered to have no single points of failure. Everything is redundant, and we can route around most network failures without anyone noticing."

"You sure made people take notice today," Raj said, without looking up from his tablet—brand new, not yet released to the public. With a Ph.D. in mathematics from M.I.T., Raj was one of the most brilliant technologists at the firm. Despite being the manager of the firm's entire Application Development Group, he still routinely wrote code himself, usually late at night, and often sparred with software developers on the finer details of their craft. He wore black dress pants and a crisply pressed white shirt, sleeves rolled up to reveal several personal tracking devices on his wrists. His thinning black hair was carefully combed to one side. His long fingers noodled his new gadget.

"You can't help but notice when you lose millions of dollars," he said. "No one can trade. Like the time we couldn't trade last week. And yesterday. And, thanks to you, we'll all certainly notice in March, when we get our bonuses."

"Get to the point," Roger said, looking at Bill.

"Yes," said Bill, glaring at Raj, who continued to tap away on his tablet without looking up. "As I was saying, we have full redundancy in our network, including our core routers."

"Explain," Roger said.

"They're the central routers that connect all parts of our network. We're careful with them. Only half of them are active at any given time, and they have enough capacity to handle all the network traffic, even on super busy days like yesterday. We keep the other half of the routers on standby; if something goes wrong, they take over automatically, like they did yesterday."

"So why the outage?"

"The problem is that four weeks ago, the vendor released an emergency security patch for the core routers. They found a vulnerability that could allow someone to take full control of the network."

"That's not good."

"It was all over the news. The router vendor found this vulnerability being exploited at Castle-Mart for the past six months—the hackers were using it to steal credit card numbers. So in response to this, we got a security patch from the vendor and installed it in our lab, to test before we did anything to the production network. We ran some load tests and everything looked fine. Then that Saturday night we installed the software on our standby routers, and cut over all the network traffic there."

"And then?"

"The upgrade seemed to go well. But just to be on the safe side, we waited two weeks before patching the rest of the routers."

"Which brings us to last Saturday."

"Right. So last Saturday night, we patched the rest of the routers. Again, everything looked good. Now all of our routers had the latest security patch installed."

"So this patch is the root cause of the outage on Monday?" asked Ollie. He was the head of the Distributed Systems Group, which managed thousands of servers the firm needed to conduct its business. Thin, with closely cropped hair and a permanent five o'clock shadow, he wore faded jeans and a rumpled T-shirt with a logo of a tech company that no longer existed.

"You of all people should know it's not so simple," Bill said. "We had this patch running in production for two weeks without any issues."

"But never with as much traffic as we had on Monday?" Ollie said.

"That's right. As I said, we did some load tests in the lab, but we never generated as much load as we had on Monday."

"Why not?" Roger said. "For months now, we've had an explicit mandate—and budget—from the E.C. to prepare for increasing trading volumes."

"We have," said Bill. "Our production routers can handle at least twice the volume we had on Monday."

"I'm confused," Roger said.

"Just let me finish, Roger," Bill said. "Our lab has a smaller version of our production routers. The real things cost millions of dollars, and it makes no sense to have them in the lab." He paused. "Well, maybe it does now. But, in any case, the load-testing equipment we have generates a whole bunch of traffic, but not as much as we had on Monday. So we have to extrapolate from lab results. Generally speaking, if things work well in the lab, they tend to work well in production."

"Well, they didn't work so well this time," Raj said, smirking.

"No, they didn't," Bill said. "And I'm guessing the way you build your apps didn't help."

Raj stopped playing with his tablet and looked up at Bill. "Don't blame me for your shitty routers."

"I'm not. I'm just saying that we've got a system here with many moving parts—with networks and servers and, yes, the code your guys write. When the volume of trades started to cross into record territory around 2 p.m. on Monday, we started to see the routers slow down. Nothing bad, but noticed alerts, so we began investigating. We logged into one of the core routers, and issued a routine status command to find out what was going on. What happened next was really strange: instead of showing the status of the router, that command apparently crashed it."

Ollie sat up.

"Turns out," Bill said, "the security patch introduced a nasty bug into the status command, which gets activated only when there's a certain amount of traffic. We didn't know it at the time, but we hit that very bug, which caused our primary core routers to crash. That caused a momentary blip on the network, and here's where your stuff comes in, Raj."

"This oughta be interesting," Raj said under his breath.

"So after there was a brief network pause while the standby router took over automatically, we started to see an exponential increase in network traffic. We couldn't figure out why this was happening because the volume of trades didn't increase. We think maybe your apps were not designed to handle network outages."

"Oh, OK, so you expect me to rewrite our entire application portfolio just because you can't keep the network up? Everywhere I've ever worked, the network functions fine no matter what—even on 9/11—except this place."

"Gentlemen," said Roger, "instead of pointing fingers at one another, why don't we focus on the root cause?"

Bill was shaken. In addition to his day job, he was a longtime volunteer EMT, and had lost friends at the World Trade Center on 9/11. Reminders of that day always hurt, but in this context, they hurt more. "The root cause..." He worked to regain his composure. "OK...Now, after the primary router crashed and the standby router took over, it started to get overloaded with all the traffic. So we again logged in, and started to troubleshoot."

"Who's 'we'?" Ollie asked.

"It was Mike, actually. He logged in and started to troubleshoot, and in the process accidentally took down the standby router using that same buggy command. That took down the entire network."

Roger closed his eyes and tapped his fingers on his forehead. "Hang on, Mike used the same command again? The one that took down the first router?"

Bill nodded.

"That's just careless," Raj said.

Bill looked at Raj angrily. "Actually, we literally use this command hundreds of times every day. We had no idea that using it would take down the network."

"It sounds like we have our root cause," Ollie said.

"What's that?" Bill said.

"If Mike didn't use that buggy command, the network wouldn't have crashed, right? I'm sure he didn't mean it, but his mistake is what caused the outage."

"I see where you're going with that, Ollie," Bill said. "Yes, it was an operator error, but"—Bill hesitated, knowing that Mike's job was on the line—"Mike is one of our most experienced engineers."

"Well, any experienced engineer knows to be extra careful when trouble-shooting in production," said Ollie. "Especially on a day with record trading volumes."

"Didn't Mike also cause the previous network outage?" Raj asked. "We almost lost our ability to trade that day. I guess we got lucky."

"Bill, didn't you talk to Mike after that first outage?" said Linda, who wasn't sitting at the table, but near the wall. She was the head of Client Services, the team that bore the brunt of calls from within the firm, and from its clients, during any outage. She wore beige slacks and a tailored white shirt, her blonde hair cut at the shoulders. She spoke with a slight, unidentifiable accent. "Didn't you have a sit-down with Mike about being more careful when working in production?"

"If you're going to throw anyone under the bus, it should be me," Bill said.

"No one is going to throw you under the bus, Bill," said Linda. "Mike is the one with a history of taking down production. He's a bit of a cowboy."

"Mike's been with the firm for six years," said Bill. "He's done amazing work. He did take down the network this time, but he also got it working again. Without him, we would have had a much longer outage. It's hard to find engineers as good as Mike, and we almost lost him earlier this year when we docked his bonus for the last outage."

The room fell silent. Finally, Roger said, "One of the core values of our firm is accountability. We have to hold people accountable for their actions. I can't see us tolerating someone who continues to make mistakes. Mike's careless mistakes are costing the firm money, and also making the entire I.T. team look incompetent." Roger, speaking to Bill, said, "I agree with Ollie. The root cause of this kerfuffle is operator error. You need to deal with it. We can't afford to have this happen again. Let me be absolutely clear: all our jobs are on the line. Given how much we're paying for talent, we should be able to find engineers who take more care. Make it happen, Bill."

Roger stood up and looked around the room. "Are there any questions?" No one said anything, so Roger left the room, followed by Raj. Linda got up next, saying "Sorry, Bill." Ollie, who was sitting next to Bill, sighed and shook his head.

Soon Bill was on his own, in a conference room overlooking Manhattan. It was a cloudless day, and Bill could see all the way downtown to where the Twin Towers once stood.

Dealing with the Root Cause

Mike was in his office, finishing up the list of steps the networking team would take to reduce the likelihood of another outage. Despite close to two decades of working in financial technology, he never got used to the outages, and the adrenaline highs and lows that came with them. No two were alike, and they were always surprising. As the amount of processing power and bandwidth required to run financial intuitions increased, so did the complexity of the systems and networks. Mike often argued with other engineers about whether humans had reached the limits of their ability to understand how these systems function and how they broke down.

The phone rang, and Mike picked it up. It was Bill.

"Hey, Mike, can you please come down to the second floor?"

Mike knew, right away, what was happening. Large financial services firms are known for the boom-and-bust mentality—binge hiring when times are good, and laying off in a series of rounds when times are bad. In his six years at the firm, Mike had seen the way that R.I.F.s—Reductions in Force—were conducted: people were called to the second floor by their manager, and wouldn't return. At the end of the day, the manager would gather the remaining team to brief them. Since "the departures" were not allowed to come back, their managers had to pack whatever remained in their offices and desks into cardboard boxes, to be shipped home.

Mike checked his firm-issued BlackBerry. It was still working. This was the only device Mike used, making him a subject of jokes from the other techies in I.T., who were always playing with the latest gadgets. Mike's whole life was on this BlackBerry—his contacts, the schedules of his kids' soccer practices. Mike scrolled through the menu on the device to turn off its radio. Disconnected from the network, the BlackBerry couldn't be used to send or receive emails, or to make phone calls. And it couldn't be wiped remotely.

Mike didn't want to make Bill wait. He looked around the office, picked up the pictures of his kids, and put them into his backpack. He and Bill had worked together before, and it was Bill who had hired him. Bill was a great boss, always willing to go to bat for his team for the right things, even those that weren't popular with others.

Mike walked out of his office, and made his way to the elevator. He noticed that he was sweating. When the doors of the elevator opened, a few of his coworkers walked out, surprised to see him there. "Banker's hours?" one of them joked. Mike winced. "I'll see you guys in a bit," he said, as the elevator doors closed.

Bill met Mike on the second floor. Mike noticed the muffled sound of his footsteps on the thick carpet as he followed Bill to a conference room. The room could easily seat 25 people around the wooden conference table, but there was no one there now except Bill and Elaine, the head of H.R. She wore a black blouse and dark-blue pants. She motioned for Mike to sit in one of the Aeron chairs across from her.

Bill closed the door and sat down next to Mike. Elaine hesitated for a moment, then spoke. "Mike, this is never easy. The firm is terminating your employment, effective today." She looked down at the folder on which she was resting her hands, and moved it across the table toward Mike. "In recognition of your years of service, the firm is prepared to offer you a severance package. You'll have seven days to review it, and return the documents to me."

She paused while Mike opened the folder and pretended to study its contents, blood rushing to his head. Bill said, "Sorry, man."

"We'd like for you to return all the firm-issued equipment," Elaine continued. "Do you have your phone and laptop with you?"

"My laptop is upstairs," Mike said, "and I forgot the BlackBerry at home today. Sorry."

"That's fine," Elaine said. "You can ship it to me later." Seeing that Mike was taking the news reasonably well, Elaine relaxed a bit. She asked Mike if he had any other questions.

"Can I take a few minutes to read over these documents?" Mike asked. "If it's the standard stuff, I should be able to sign them here. No reason to postpone it."

"Of course," Elaine said, standing up. "Why don't I give you a few minutes?"

Bill stood up as well, and offered Mike his hand. "Good luck, man. And thanks for all your hard work. I'm sure I'll see you soon, and of course, you let me know how I can help." Mike shook Bill's hand, and watched both Bill and Elaine leave the room. It was only then that he noticed two security guards standing just outside the conference room.

I already took down the network, Mike thought. What more can I do?

Operator Error

Owing to its location across the street from the firm's headquarters, O'Gradys was such a part of the social fabric of the firm that it was referred to as "the dining room." As Linda made her way to the second floor of the bar, she nodded and waved to her colleagues packed in small groups around tall tables cluttered with beer glasses.

The second floor was far more subdued. Linda saw Bill and Ollie sitting across from each other in a booth. As she slid into her seat next to Ollie, Bill was shaking his head.

"The thing that makes absolutely no sense is, does anyone really believe that now that Mike is gone, we're never going to have network outages?"

"Of course not," said Ollie.

"We're not even a little bit less likely to have these incidents," Bill continued. "In fact, we've just fired the guy who knows the most about our network."

"He's certainly the expert in these particular incidents, having caused them," said Ollie.

"You're right. Mike was the guy who could have made the network better and more resistant to these types of errors."

"No one is arguing that Mike was a great engineer," said Linda. "But we have to hold people accountable for their actions."

"What does that even mean, 'accountable'?" Bill said, a little too loudly.

Linda was taken aback by Bill's anger. "You know what it means. We need to hold someone responsible so that people think twice before doing these kinds of things again."

"Which kinds of things?" Bill asked.

"Is there any disagreement," Linda said, "that it was Mike who took down the network more than once?"

"Yes, he did take down the network," Bill said, "but not on purpose. He wasn't being malicious—he was trying to do his job. The best job he could, given what he knew at the time. He was trying to fix it, not to make it worse. It was an accident."

"An accident that cost the firm money," Linda said. "He should have been more careful, since he knew he was working on our live network."

"Mike is one of the most careful and experienced engineers that I've ever worked with. Strangely, no one is talking about all the times that Mike kept the network running."

"Again," Linda said, "the point is, Mike took down the network. He's responsible for that. He caused this outage."

"Is he the root cause, though?" asked Bill, staring at Linda.

Linda shifted in her seat. "I guess he is. Without Mike and what he did, we wouldn't have had this outage. As you said to Roger, it was an 'operator error,' and Mike is unquestionably the operator here."

"Ah, right," Bill said. "'Operator error.' That's just something that sounds like a good answer to Roger's question of who we're going to fire. So the logic goes, if Mike's the root cause, the operator, let's fire him, and we'll never have network outages again."

"Well, we'll have outages, just not outages caused by Mike."

"That's right," Bill said, "they'll be caused by other engineers being 'careless and irresponsible,' as Roger says. In fact, I won't be surprised if we have an outage similar to this one in the future. Any other engineer, regardless of experience, would have made the same mistake that Mike did. I can't even call it a mistake; he was doing the right thing—the thing that normally works—but it didn't work as expected under these particular circumstances."

"OK, Bill. So if Mike—or operator error—are not the root cause, what is?" asked Ollie.

"I don't know, Ollie," Bill said. "But one thing is for sure: if there is a single root cause, we haven't found it yet, and I don't know if we will."

Ollie's eyes narrowed. "What do you mean, *if* there is a root cause? Things don't happen randomly, right? You can't be an engineer without believing in cause and effect."

The Bad Apples

Bill finished the last of his beer, and carefully set the glass on the table. "I would love to live in a world where we could find root causes for everything. That would be so great. Unfortunately, I live in the real world where things are messy."

Bill took out a car key from his pocket and placed it in the middle of the table. "Let's ignore the electronic parts of this key for a second. Imagine it's a key to an old-fashioned car. We can hold it, we can view it from all sides, and, most importantly, we can reason about the way that it works. We can hold a very simple mental model of the key in our heads.

"Now let's think about a car. It has a lot more parts than just this key. It's considerably more complicated than the key, but it's still possible to know pretty much all there is to know about the car—especially if it's an antique one, like a Model T. A good mechanic, after working with these cars for a while, could build a pretty realistic mental model of how they function and break down. It would be considerably more nuanced than the mental model for the key, because it might have to deal with external realities like the weather, or the type of fuel that could affect the functioning of the car. But it would match the complexity of the car itself. The way that the mechanic would think about a complicated antique car would be sufficiently complicated."

"Wouldn't you say," Linda interrupted, "that Mike is like an experienced mechanic? He knew all there is to know about routers, right? And that's what makes his actions so unforgivable."

"If we only choose to think about routers, disconnected from anything else, then you're probably right. But the outage we lived through was not just about routers. Our systems are like a whole bunch of Model Ts, and every other kind of vehicle running on a 12-lane highway on the hottest day of the year. Our ability to fully understand how this complex system functions is diminished, as is our ability to control the system."

"Just because it's difficult, do we give up trying to understand?" Linda asked. "Let's say there's an accident, which causes some traffic to back up on the highway..."

"That's a great example!" Bill interrupted. "Why did this accident happen?"

"Maybe the driver had too much to drink, or maybe the driver was distracted?"

"Maybe. But why? Why was the driver drunk or distracted?"

"Well, who knows and who cares? All we care about is that we find and prosecute the person who caused it, if that person was breaking the law."

"If we can establish beyond a shadow of a doubt," Bill said, "that that person was breaking the law, and punish him—and that's all we do—then we didn't go deeply enough to understand the complex system that we're part of every time we drive. Maybe we've found someone to blame for the accident. But we still don't know *how* he was able to do it, what were the conditions that allowed the accident to occur. And even if we've removed him from the road, we've learned nothing that could make driving safer for anyone else who drives in the future."

"I disagree." Linda said. "The roads would be much safer for everyone if certain people weren't allowed to drive."

"What you're saying," Bill said, "is that the cause of the accident and the traffic jam thereafter is this driver. Remove him from the road, and you don't have that accident and its aftermath. Remove dangerous drivers and our roads automatically get safer. This is such a comfortable story, the story of how there are a few bad apples that we need to prevent from causing trouble. But how do we identify them, especially before they do something bad? Is there a gene for recklessness? Do we take away the driver's licenses of anyone who has ever been in an accident?"

"That doesn't sound crazy for drunk drivers."

"I think we do that already, but I'm not sure it does much to prevent the next drunk driver from getting behind the wheel. If someone decides to get behind the wheel drunk at 4 o'clock in the morning and there are no other cars on the road, would there be an accident? And, conversely, what about the sober, experienced driver who has an accident because of some other condition like poor visibility due to fog, or a car malfunction, or due to the way that an intersection is built?"

Bill continued. "Context is important, Linda. Imagine a man is caught speeding, and also talking on his cell phone. Clearly he's breaking at least two laws."

"Yes, and he should be fined for breaking them," Linda said.

"Now imagine he's speeding and talking on the cell phone. The policeman who stops him sees that the man's wife is in the backseat, in labor. The man is rushing to the hospital and is on the phone with the doctor."

"Well, in that case, he should get a police escort to the hospital."

"That's why we don't have robots to blindly apply the law and dole out punishment. In this case, it would actually be reckless for the police officer to arrest the husband. In this context, the husband is doing something that is reasonable, even though he might be breaking the law. He's not trying to cause an accident, he just wants to get his wife to the hospital as quickly and safely as possible."

"I think I see the point you're trying to make, Bill," said Ollie. "It has to do with intention. Most people don't set out to deliberately cause accidents, or for that matter, to take down networks. Most people come to work to do a good job. But what about people who seem to make more mistakes than others, or who repeatedly make the same mistake? And what if, despite their best intentions, they cause harm?"

"The fact that someone who's drunk even has the ability to start a car," Bill said, "has a lot to do with the harm that they can cause. What if cars wouldn't start if their driver was impaired?"

Linda nodded. "Our roads would be a lot safer."

"They would be," Bill said. "But instead of learning from the accidents and from the people involved in them—instead of taking these opportunities to understand more fully these complex systems and to make them safer and more resilient—we jump to some quick conclusion, label somebody the root cause, and get rid of them or punish them."

Holding to Account

Ollie shifted in his seat, uncomfortably. "The way things are going," he spoke slowly, "we're all going to be out of jobs soon enough."

"The firings will continue until morale improves," said Linda.

"The firings will continue until there are no humans left," said Bill, "and their human errors will no longer break our beautifully designed systems."

"I know you're kidding, Bill," said Ollie. "But when was the last time that we had a big outage, and we didn't manage to find somebody to blame?"

"Or, as we say, 'hold accountable,'" Bill said, raising his hands to make air quotes.

"All the while, accountability has nothing to do with punishment," said Ollie. "Accountability and punishment are mutually exclusive."

"That's a pretty strong statement, Ollie," said Linda. "We may not want to fire anybody, but we do need to make sure these things don't happen again."

"Wouldn't you say that in order for these things not to happen again, we need to understand what happened?"

"Well, of course—that's why we do postmortems."

"How likely are you to share the full story of what happened, if your job is on the line? Especially the bits that might get you fired?"

"Well, it's my job to say what happened, and it would be worse if I held something back and it came to light later. I see what you mean, but I don't think it happens that much here."

"Really?" Bill said. He was surprised by how loud his words came out, and lowered his voice. "I didn't hear Raj talk too much about the role of his applications in the last outage. We got our sacrificial lamb, and that was that."

"What do you mean?" asked Linda. "You yourself had said that Mike's actions caused the outage."

"But remember what I said in the meeting? That when the primary core router crashed, and when the traffic started flowing through the standby router, it started to increase exponentially? We still don't have a good explanation for that, though I suspect it had at least something to do with how applications were handling the failover. The thing is, without Raj's help, we won't be able to find out."

"I'm sure this isn't the only bit of information that wasn't fully disclosed," Ollie said. "Perhaps not consciously or maliciously, but this is exactly what we get when we look for a single root cause, which is usually someone to blame, shame, demote, or otherwise punish."

"Come to think of it," Ollie continued, "even in serious legal cases, when it's more important to find out what happened, or who's involved, immunity is offered in exchange for information."

"Holding someone accountable," Bill said, "means having them provide a full account of what happened. Full accountability is not possible with blame. We can only pick one—accountability or punishment."

"But what if someone did something maliciously?" asked Linda.

"You said it yourself," Bill said. "If we want to learn as fully as possible what happened—what is broken in the organization that allowed this person to act maliciously—threatening them may not be the answer. In any case, the vast majority of people who work here are not malicious—they're trying to do a good job. When things break, as they invariably do, why treat them like criminals? Why blame and threaten punishment for trying to do the best they can in a complex and often unpredictable world?"

Why Things Break

"I'm not convinced," said Linda, "that we can get rid of blame and punishment at the firm. It seems so ingrained in how we do things. It's the flip side of reward— you get rewarded for not screwing up."

"You get rewarded," said Bill, "at least in part, for not being fully accountable."

"It's a reflection of our misunderstanding of how complex systems function," said Ollie. "Failure is a normal part of complex systems, yet it's always so surprising when they fail. Why aren't we more surprised when they function?"

"Failure is normal?" said Linda, raising her eyebrows.

"In complex systems," Ollie replied, "failure is absolutely normal and expected. Malfunction is as 'normal' as 'regular' functioning."

"That makes no sense, Ollie!"

"OK, let's get a little philosophical for a minute." Ollie said. "Why do things break?"

"It seems that you're saying that things break because they do—that it's just normal," Linda said.

"There are lots of reasons that things break," Bill said. "Somebody does something, wear and tear, an 'Act of God.' It's not like there's a single root cause for all failures."

"Well, what if I said that there is a single root cause for all failures," Ollie said, smiling. "And for all successes, too. There's something that all systems— working or breaking—have in common, and that's change."

"Sure," Bill said, "I can see that when things break, somebody usually changes something, like a router configuration, and all hell breaks loose. But once you have a system that's functioning, the last thing you want is for someone to muck with it."

"Any system that's functioning is, in fact, changing," Ollie said. "A system needs to change in order to function. But most of the time we're not aware of the changes. For instance, right now, as I'm speaking, my vocal cords are vibrating, and my tongue is moving, and the sound of my voice is traveling to your ears and vibrating your eardrums, which are sending signals to your brain, which is converting them into information that you can understand. Then it's storing it in your memory. That's just a sliver of what's happening at this moment. But you can see that all these processes require change, which is constant. Without change, our communication would be impossible."

Bill sat up. "I've never thought of it that way. Even in computing, it's all zeros changing into ones and back again. Without change, computing would be impossible."

"Exactly!" said Ollie. "But wait, there's something even more fundamental! Why is change possible?"

Ollie looked at Bill and Linda, who were contemplating his question.

"Not sure what you mean," said Bill. "Maybe getting a bit too philosophical for me, man."

Ollie said, "What I'm saying is, there's something that enables change, and that is required for change: that is, the fact that things are *changeable*. It's their basic, fundamental property."

"Things change because they're changeable?" said Bill, puzzled.

"Perhaps a better way to say it is that all things are impermanent. And it's not just me saying it—it's the nature of the world we live in. Twenty-five-hundred years ago, the Buddha said that all compounded phenomena are impermanent."

"Compounded?" asked Linda.

"'Compounded' meaning 'consisting of two or more things,'" Ollie replied. "And I think we can all agree that the systems we work with consist of more than two parts!"

"That's for sure," said Bill, smiling. "So things break because of impermanence, and there's not a thing that we can do about it."

"They function because of impermanence, too," said Ollie. "In fact, if we had to pick a single root cause for all failures *and* successes, it would be impermanence."

"It's certainly not very satisfying to blame impermanence for an outage," said Linda. "You can't hold impermanence responsible. Doesn't seem useful at all."

"It's not," said Ollie. "It's useful only as a reminder that if we ever find a root cause of any outage that's not impermanence, we'll know that it's just an illusion and wishful thinking."

"So if there's no root cause," said Linda, "do things just happen randomly?"

"If things did happen randomly," Ollie replied, "we might as well give up and go home. If we planted a seed, and sometimes it grew into a plant, assuming the right conditions, of course, and sometimes it grew into a bicycle..."

Bill interrupted Ollie. "Assuming the right conditions? How do we know what conditions are right?"

"That's precisely what we do—whether we're scientists or engineers or farmers or even philosophers—we try to figure out which set of conditions gets us the desired outcome, at least more often than not. We can't possibly know all the conditions, and the ones we do know are not always in our control."

"You mean the butterfly effect?" asked Bill.

"Exactly! Maybe one of the reasons—one of the conditions—of the outage we just had was some butterfly fluttering its wings somewhere in Africa."

"And sometimes it's someone like Mike fluttering the keyboard keys," added Linda, mimicking Ollie's intonation. "Again, you can't hold that butterfly responsible. How is that helpful or useful?"

"It's useful because it more accurately describes the world we live in. If you want a simplistic view of the real world, you can always blame the humans for screwing up. And while you might feel better having found the culprit—the so-called 'root cause'—this nice and comfortable story is complete fiction. It won't help us prevent future accidents."

"So what will?"

"Learning from both failures and successes. Feeding these learnings as signals back into the system, which will change and adapt to this new information. That's why air travel has become as safe as it is over time—every time there is an accident or near-accident, it's investigated, and the results are fed back into the system. This system includes air craft, traffic control, weather, engineers, and so on."

"Given all this impermanence—" Bill said, "the constant change, the unpredictable conditions—it's a wonder that we're able to build homes that don't fall down, airplanes that don't crash, and trading systems that work."

"And one of the reasons for that is that the people who build and work in these complex systems are exceptionally good at learning what works and doesn't. They're good at adapting quickly and continually. We have this amazing ability to make sense of these complex systems, and to do what makes sense at the time. We deserve at least as much credit for when things go well, as blame for when things fail."

"I'll drink to that!" said Bill, raising his empty glass and looking around for someone to refill it.

7

Who's to Blame?

"Hi, Mom," said Andrew to Linda as she opened the front door of her house. Andrew didn't look up from his homework, which was spread out on the table in the dining room.

"Why are you still up?" Linda asked, with hints of frustration and resignation. She took off her shoes and walked to the dining room. She had a sinking feeling that whatever was about to happen would end in tears.

"Because I'm bad at math," Andrew said.

Linda sat down next to her son, noticing that he was now almost as tall as she. His eyes were red and his thick, black hair was standing up in all directions. "A hairstyle like an explosion at a macaroni factory," they joked when his hair got this disheveled, but this was no time for joking. The table had tiny bits of rubber strewn about it, the result of furious, frustrated erasing that Andrew would do during his math homework.

From an early age, Andrew seemed exceptionally gifted at words and languages. He started speaking his first language, Bosnian, relatively late, but everyone marveled at the fully formed sentences that he spoke when he was four. He knew no English when he entered kindergarten, but within a few weeks was able to communicate with his teachers and classmates with ease.

Math was another story.

"Mom, I need help!" Andrew said.

Linda could almost predict what would happen next, because it had happened so many times before. She would try to explain whatever math concept her son was having trouble with, and he would try again and still get it wrong. "It's so simple!" Linda would say, trying to remain calm. "Just follow the instructions!" Andrew would become exasperated and say, "It's simple for you, Mom! I just don't get it. I'm so bad at math!"

Linda wouldn't say anything, but she agreed. Andrew was bad at math. Linda had excelled at math in her school days. She surprised her parents and teachers with just how good she was, and became a regular participant in math Olympiads, winning the one in Sarajevo in the ninth grade. Linda studied computer engineering in college, and eventually became a software developer. Because math came so easily to her—the same math that so easily drove her son to tears—she wondered if there was something wrong with Andrew. Was he lazy? Was he just not persistent enough? He was so easily frustrated, and made the same mistakes over and over again.

Linda thought about the conversation at the bar from earlier that night. Operator error. Yes, Mike made the error, and made the same error again. It was unfortunate, and it was also not about Mike. Mike was not being careless, and he certainly wasn't lazy. If anything, Mike was sensible, thoughtful, methodical—a real engineer. He did what made sense to him at the time, and found out later that it was the wrong thing. He wasn't trying to take the network down.

And Andrew wasn't trying to fail at math. He didn't want to keep making the same mistakes, and he too was just doing what made sense, which turned out to be the wrong thing. Was there something about the textbook, or the way that Andrew was taught at school, or even the way that Linda was teaching him? All these things compounded and conspired against him, resulting in her only son sobbing in frustration at half past 10 on a school night.

Linda put her arm around the boy, and drew him close to her. For the first time, she felt that "Andrew is just bad at math" was a deeply unsatisfactory explanation for what she was witnessing. It was much deeper, and much more complex.

"I'm sorry," she whispered in Andrew's ear. "I'm so, so sorry." She held him close, as he cried. "You're not bad at math. It's not you. I can see how hard you're working. I can only imagine how frustrating it feels."

8

Trade-offs

It took Bill a moment to realize that a policeman was motioning him to approach. Puzzled, he took the earbuds from his ears and walked to the sidewalk where the officer, who was very tall, and his much shorter partner were standing.

"Can I see some I.D.?" the tall one said in an unmistakably Brooklyn accent.

"Why?" asked Bill.

"You see that road right there?" asked the officer, pointing to the one that Bill had just crossed. Bill nodded. "You see that light right there? You, Sir, were observed jaywalking. I.D., please."

Although Bill had always lived just north of the city, he had spent all of his working life in Manhattan. His commute, with the exceptions of weather-related delays, was timed and polished to a shine, putting him in his office at 7 o'clock sharp every weekday morning. The tail end of his trip to work involved a walk from the subway station toward this street. Without thinking, he would look around and cross the street if there were no cars, regardless of the traffic light's color.

Bill often joked that you could always spot tourists in New York—they were the ones standing at the pedestrian crossing, waiting for the silhouette to light up white on the traffic signal, while the true New Yorkers rushed right past them. One of the reasons that Bill commuted so early was because the city at that time was blissfully empty of tourists, and he could move at native New Yorker speed.

Bill took his thick leather wallet from his back pocket and handed his driver's license to the cop. "I'm an E.M.T.," he volunteered.

"Good for you!" the cop said without skipping a beat. He handed the I.D. to his partner, who was already writing out the details of the summons on the form. "You, of all people, should know not to jaywalk."

"You're giving me a ticket for jaywalking?" Bill asked. He was both surprised and amused. *Of all things, a jaywalking ticket?*

"Sir, let me put it to you this way," the officer offered, cordially. "Last weekend, a young lady was jaywalking across this very street, just like you; listening to her headphones, just like you. Didn't see the delivery truck going at 35 miles an hour uptown. He had the green light, by the way, just like the cars did when you were walking. Then boom!" the officer said, smashing his fist into the palm of his other hand. "Hit. And. Run." He pointed to the camera attached to the traffic light. "We caught the guy, but that ain't gonna help him, and it sure as hell ain't gonna help the lady neither."

"What happened to the lady?" Bill asked.

"She passed in the hospital."

The officer's partner finished writing out the ticket, and with a practiced efficiency, executed the next series of actions: pen clicked closed, pen placed in pocket, ticket folded in half, ticket handed to Bill. "Have a nice day," he said, and both the officers headed off downtown.

Bill studied the ticket, looking for the amount of the fine, then quickly put it away inside his jacked. *How curious*, he thought. *I've never gotten a jaywalking ticket, and I've pretty much been jaywalking every single day, several times a day!* Then he remembered a conversation he recently had with Ollie, something about trade-offs between efficiency and thoroughness, and how humans are especially good at continually making these trade-offs.

I guess all these years I was more concerned about how quickly I could get to the office than with getting there safely (or at least without jaywalking tickets). Although I always checked for cars, I never waited for the WALK signal. And I certainly never looked for cops on the street.

And then Bill thought about the cops, who—impressed with a recent, unnecessary death of a young woman—probably got the instructions to "serve and protect" by giving out jaywalking tickets. *Well, it certainly won't bring the lady back—or eradicate jaywalking—but at least I'll be looking out for cops before crossing the street. I guess that'll count as me being more thorough!*

He thought of Mike. *Was Mike making a trade-off, trying to get the network restored as quickly as he could, and in the process not thinking through what was happening thoroughly? If he slowed down, would he have made the same mistake?*

Bill took out his smartphone and typed a message to Ollie: "Just got a ticket for jaywalking!" He stopped walking, considering for a moment whether he was investing in efficiency over thoroughness again. He continued his message to Ollie: "must discuss trade-offs wrt outage," and pressed the Send button.

9

Reliable Errors (or Reliably Error-Prone)

"You ought to get it framed," said Ollie, examining the jaywalking ticket that Bill put on his desk. "It's like a two-dollar bill—lucky and rare."

"Coffee?" Bill asked, smiling. "Downstairs?"

"And talk about trade-offs again?" Ollie replied, getting up from his seat. "I thought you'd never ask! After you, Sir!"

As they walked toward the elevators, Ollie said, "E.T.T.O. is efficiency-thoroughness trade-off. You know, Professor Erik Hollnagel's idea."

"Right. I was just thinking about that," Bill said. "Hollnagel noticed that you can't have both efficiency and thoroughness, and that we have to continually balance between the two. For instance, you can say that in some sense before 9/11, the transportation safety folks favored efficiency. You could whisk through baggage check in 5 minutes, without having to take your shoes off!"

Ollie cut in. "But after 9/11, we swing deeply into thoroughness territory, maybe too much. So now we might be moving in the direction of efficiency again."

"I was thinking about Mike," Bill said. "And how he was making these trade-offs during the outage."

"Definitely," Ollie said. "We've all been there: there's a fire—literal or figurative—and we have to make a split-second decision about whether to put it out the fast way, or"—Ollie made air quotes—"'the right way.' The dirty little secret here is that we make decisions in real time, but evaluate them with the benefit of hindsight. Whether a decision (like a particular trade-off) was correct can be determined only in retrospect."

"That doesn't feel right," said Bill. "There are rules and laws. There are procedures. There are even best practices, in some cases. I think I know most of the time if I'm making the right decision."

"We'd all like to believe that we know. How about the jaywalking incident? You were clearly breaking the law. It was only a matter of time before your wrong decisions caught up with you. I'm just glad you didn't get hit by a bus."

Bill looked confused. Ollie smiled and said, "Look, Bill, you did what made sense at the time. Until today, no one ever ran you over, and you never got caught. Your decision to jaywalk seemed totally reasonable before you got a ticket. And now that you've got to pay a fine, how does your decision look?"

"Kind of stupid, actually. I feel like I should have known better."

"Good news, Bill!" said Ollie. "We ran some tests, and found that you've contracted a case of the hindsight bias!"

"I didn't know it was contagious!"

"That's right," Ollie said in the voice of a 1950s television announcer. "Colloquially known as 'hindsight 20/20,' or the 'Monday morning quarterback syndrome,' it affects everyone. There is no known cure, so we would all do well to practice mental hygiene to reduce the risk of spreading this serious disease. When you decided to jaywalk, did you know that you would get fined?"

"No, but I knew I could have been."

"I doubt it was top of mind. That's just the hindsight bias talking, and it's tricking you into thinking that something that is obvious now was also obvious then. But it wasn't."

"What?"

"Look, Bill," Ollie continued. "Do you think that Mike knew that what he was about to do in order to troubleshoot the network would take it down?"

"Probably not."

"Probably? Are you saying that Mike might have purposefully taken down the network?"

"No, of course not. It was an accident. I'm just saying that he should have been more careful."

"So, again, that's hindsight bias. Mike didn't know that something bad was about to happen. He didn't have the information we now have, and it wasn't obvious to him at the time—and he *was* being appropriately careful."

"OK, Ollie, that makes sense. So how do you tell if your thinking is affected by hindsight bias—or other biases?"

"Daniel Kahneman—one of the people who's been studying these cognitive biases since the seventies—says that it's easier to spot biases in others than in ourselves. Since you've asked, I'm happy to share what I know, and remind you when you might be affected. I do fully expect you to return the favor in the future."

Ollie went on, "Anytime you hear 'didn't,' 'could have,' 'if only,' or 'should have,' you can be pretty sure that whoever is saying them is under the influence of hindsight bias. These phrases are called 'counterfactuals'—they describe, literally, what didn't happen. The future is uncertain, but we can't change the past. 'If only Mike didn't troubleshoot the router,' for example, is not describing what actually happened, and instead of learning from the past, we're engaging in a kind of lazy (but very comforting) wishful thinking. 'Mike could have asked for help,' or 'Mike should have done more testing in the lab,' or 'Mike didn't do the right thing,' are all counterfactuals, and are all evidence of hindsight bias. When we think in this way, we forget what Mike did, in fact, do. More important, if we get stuck there when investigating past events, we never fully understand what really happened, and we can't learn why what Mike did made absolute sense at the time.

"And without learning," Bill said, "we have no chance of making any improvements."

Now in the cafeteria, the two men filled their Styrofoam cups with a hot, murky liquid the cafeteria called "coffee."

"In hindsight," Bill said, "I'll probably regret drinking this, and wonder why I didn't just go across the street to get a better cup of coffee."

"And yet," said Ollie, "it makes perfect sense right now, doesn't it? This coffee is closer and cheaper, and will do the job."

"OK," said Bill, "so that's hindsight bias. It sounds like to counteract it, we have to listen for counterfactuals, and then mentally transport ourselves back in time to see what was actually known or obvious at the time?"

"Much easier said than done. But if we are to learn from the past—from both failures and successes—it's precisely what we have to do."

Bill and Ollie paid for their coffees and walked in silence toward the elevator.

"How many other biases are there?" Bill asked.

"Many," said Ollie. "Kahneman's book, *Thinking Fast and Slow*—which is mostly about biases—is 500 pages long, and doesn't even cover half of them. There are close to 200 listed in Wikipedia. Cognitive biases, in general, are mistakes that we make pretty reliably, and most of the time we're unaware that we're making them. And the biases travel in packs.

"Take, for instance, outcome bias, which is almost always there when we experience hindsight bias. With outcome bias, we judge the quality of decisions made in the past given the outcome, which, of course, is unknown at decision time. Imagine there was no outage last week. Would we think differently about the quality of Mike's decisions?"

"Well, I'm not sure Mike would have gotten promoted," Bill said, "but he surely wouldn't have gotten fired."

"The flip side of outcome bias is that it can lead us to hero worship—celebrating people who made pretty bad or risky decisions that somehow still turned out all right."

"Well, there's plenty of that going on around Wall Street! The ends, after all, justify the means—unless you get caught."

"The outcomes reliably color our perception. And, as with any bias, we mostly don't know we're being influenced with outcome bias, which means that we'll have a pretty hard time sorting out the good decisions from the bad."

"Or good *people* from the bad?"

"Ah, yes, that brings me to my personal favorite bias—fundamental attribution error—which results in exactly the leap that you just took from the individuals' actions and decisions to the individuals themselves. For instance, when I talk to you, especially before you've had your first cup of coffee, I might get the distinct impression that you're a pretty grumpy guy."

"Who, me?" Bill said, smiling.

"In this situation," Ollie continued, "if I were under the influence of fundamental attribution error, I would think of this grumpiness as part of your personality, instead of attributing it to a lack of caffeine in your system."

"Anyone who works with networks—or complex systems in general—has the right to be at least a little bit grumpy, don't you think?"

Ollie laughed. "Indeed! And as long as we attribute their behavior to their conditions, we're good. The moment we attribute it to their personality, we're making fundamental attribution error. That's precisely how Mike becomes 'careless'—we're forgetting the circumstances, the stress, and the decision fatigue that he was experiencing when he was working through the outage. Oddly, whenever we think of ourselves, we have no problem seeing our actions and moods as a result of our surroundings, and not tying them to ourselves too tightly."

"I have to say, Ollie, you're blowing my mind right now. I am guilty of all these biases!"

"We all are," Ollie said. "And there's more of them—a lot more. Kahneman, for one, is not optimistic about our ability to spot them in ourselves. Which is why it's important for us to learn to spot them in one another, as well as give each other permission to name the biases when we see them."

"Well, for what it's worth, I not only give you permission, but request that you call me out when you see me under the influence of any bias."

"I'll try. And please do the same for me. It'll take some practice for all of us. When trying to learn from the things that happened in the past, we have to mentally transport ourselves to the past, and continually ask ourselves, 'What was known at the time? How did the decision make sense? What circumstances were influencing my decisions? What conditions were present that enabled me to act in a particular way? How did I know what I knew, and how did I do what I did?' Maybe then we can learn something useful."

The Second Victim

"How do you think I'm doing?" Mike shot back at Bill. They were sitting across from each other at a diner not far from Mike's house. It was Saturday, and they'd just ordered breakfast. Then Mike sighed, and said, "I'm sorry for snapping. It's just that it felt pretty awful to have my career at the firm end that way."

"We've been talking a lot about you," Bill said. "Linda and Ollie and I."

"Yeah?"

"And also about what happened—the outage. We're learning that we haven't been dealing with outages in the best ways. Or with our people."

"Really? I just keep replaying it in my head, and all that I can come up with is, 'What a stupid mistake!' I've been doing this for close to 20 years, and I behaved like a total newbie. I totally deserved being fired. I would have probably resigned in shame anyway."

"I hear you, Mike. I've been there myself, both in my career and as an E.M.T. Thinking, 'If only I got there a minute earlier, I could have saved her.' Or seeing in retrospect so clearly what I should have done, and feeling like an idiot for not doing it."

"That pretty much sums up how I'm doing."

"But here's the thing, Mike—a few things, actually. Do you think anyone would have done anything different from what you did?"

Mike turned toward the window, which overlooked a busy highway. He was still for a few moments before speaking. "Well, who knows? I guess I'm glad it was me, and not any of the guys."

"Mike, the one thing I'm sure of is that if it weren't for you, it would have taken us a lot longer to recover. And I also know that pretty much anyone would have done what you did. I mean, you did everything right. You had no idea—no one had any idea—that it would blow up. No one had any clue!"

"Yeah, well, I sure could have been more careful. I could have stopped to think. I could have connected that using the router status command would brick the router. I could have done more testing before rolling out the patch."

"But, in fact, you didn't do any of these things, and no amount of wishful thinking now would have helped back then. Also, don't forget that you were under a ton of pressure—it's not like you had all day to figure things out, what with the firm losing its ability to trade all of a sudden. In reality, you did what any experienced engineer would do: log in and look around. Who knew that the very act of looking would have this effect? It's some kind of Schrödinger's router, man!"

Mike nodded in agreement, a hint of a smile appearing on his lips. "Yeah, there was an extremely unlikely, black swan event hiding in the system, waiting for just the right set of conditions to manifest."

"And once the system broke down," Bill said, "we adapted and brought it back to life. We learned a bit more about the system, and we made it a bit more resilient. But not as much as if you were still there. I consider letting you go to be one of the biggest mistakes of my career."

"Wow, Bill, it means a lot to me to hear you say that. I knew that it wasn't entirely your choice. I know how the firm deals with people who lose them money."

"Yeah, we've been talking about that a whole bunch, too—our culture of blame and punishment. Ollie thinks it's even risker than any kind of technical issue. And I agree."

"Really?"

"Well, it leads to the covering up of important information. Which leads to even more fragility. I think the type of black swan event that could happen here won't just lose the firm money, but might put it out of business entirely. Who knows what types of risks are not being disclosed when people are afraid to speak up."

"I've never thought about it that way. I've always been honest about my screwups, and assumed everyone else was, too. But that's probably a naïve assumption."

"People want to do the right thing, Mike, but sometimes our culture gets in the way. I think Raj and his folks could share more of their side of the outage. But I can't blame them for not volunteering the information. That's why in my E.M.T. squad, you literally can't be prosecuted based on the information you disclose during a postmortem. It's treated as privileged information. And unlike the postmortems at the firm, ours sometimes involve dead people."

"So you can't get fired from your volunteer E.M.T. role?" Mike asked.

"It's great to see you smiling, man," said Bill. "To answer your question, you can't be prosecuted as long as you provide a full account of what happened. That's the real meaning of 'accountability.'"

"I didn't know that. Why does your town do that?"

"So that we can learn fully, and improve at our jobs, which means saving and helping more people in the future."

"Huh!"

"One more thing," said Bill. "Blame has two sides. One is when we blame others—it does give us a sort of satisfaction, as long as the story we've constructed is nice and believable. But there's another side to blame, and that's blaming ourselves, or accepting blame from others. Sometimes when accidents happen, we hear about the victims—the people who die or are injured. But there is often a second victim—whoever we blame for the accident. Even if they're not prosecuted, they sometimes get really depressed or worse. And I get a sense that you haven't exactly been taking the whole thing well."

"You think?" Mike said. "No, I haven't. I've been taking it pretty hard. But don't worry; I'll be OK. I'm sure there's a silver lining in here somewhere."

"You've got a lot to be proud of, Mike. You worked through a nasty outage, and you got the firm back to trading. You provided a full account of what happened, despite the personal risk. You acted professionally when you were let go. You took full responsibility, and I think you took a bunch of blame, which you didn't need to take. You don't have to be a second victim."

Mike looked directly at Bill with a hint of a smile. He took a padded envelope from the seat beside him, and put it on the table, resting his right hand on it. "In the spirit of accountability, I made a quick decision the day of the outage to keep my BlackBerry for a few extra days because I wanted to sync my personal contacts and calendar before the device was wiped. I take full responsibility for my actions, and I have now provided a full account of what happened. And I take none of the blame."

Mike paused, still looking directly at Bill. He slid the envelope toward Bill and said, "Will you please make sure this gets to Elaine?"

"I will," Bill said, smiling.

The Downside of Blame

"Do you have a minute?" asked Ollie, poking his head into Raj's office.

"Come in, buddy," said Raj in a welcoming tone. "Sit down. What's on your mind?"

Almost two decades ago, fresh out of college, both Ollie and Raj had met as trainees in the yearlong Technology Analyst Program at Waterstone. They were not exactly great friends, and did not spend much time together socially. Still, they kept in touch after they left Waterstone, and through the years had developed a habit of speaking honestly and openly with each other.

"I'm wondering who's next," Ollie said.

"Mike was our sacrificial lamb," Raj replied without skipping a beat. "The gods are sated for a while. It's not important. Why are you crying over spilt milk, buddy?"

"The next time it could be someone on your team. Or you. Or me."

Raj raised his brows, revealing deep wrinkles on his forehead.

"Don't you think," Ollie continued, "that if we have an outage or some kind of malfunction tied to your group, that Roger and the E.C. will demand another head?"

"That's how our world works. Are you really surprised? Do you remember our mantra from T.A.P.?"

"'Don't Fuck Up.' Might as well have it tattooed. They've certainly taught us that—don't fuck up, and you won't be kicked out of T.A.P. Don't fuck up, and you'll have a long career on the street. Just don't fuck up. Do you remember that D.B.A., the one who took down one of the market data feeds and then tried to erase the database logs so he wouldn't get fired?"

"Certainly didn't help him," Raj said.

"No, it didn't. And what did we all learn? Did we learn how not to take down data feeds?"

"My friend, we learned an even more valuable lesson: Don't get caught!"

"Cover your ass better. That's the main skill we learned. Not how to make our systems or organizations more resilient."

"Look, buddy, nobody ever got a bonus for causing an outage. That's just how this world works. That's not what we're paid to do."

"Our incentives are making our systems fragile."

"How so?"

"When something goes wrong, we're quick to find the so-called root cause, which is usually just shorthand for 'Who fucked up?' And even if that person doesn't get fired, the possibility is always in the air. It stops us from learning about the deeper underlying conditions for outages, or even what's needed to make things work. So here we are, stuck with a kindergarten-level understanding, complete with tooth fairies and Santa Claus. Blame is the frigid, arctic air that stunts the development of a deeper understanding of our systems, which is the only way we can really improve them."

"I'm not sure I follow, exactly."

"You have a headache," Ollie said, "you take aspirin, and it goes away for a while, but you never find out if it was a change in the weather or a tumor that caused the headache. We're just treating the symptoms instead of getting a C.A.T. scan and finding out what's wrong."

Raj nodded slowly.

"In our case," Ollie continued, "these outages are symptoms of trouble somewhere deeper in our organization. Our postmortems are superficial, not diagnostic. Our remedies are placebos, which might not even make us feel better. We're more like witchdoctors on a witch hunt."

"Buddy, I don't have time to dig deeper."

"We can save a lot of time by not firing people."

"I don't like firing people. Nobody does. But you're talking about changing the culture of this place, of Wall Street. I'm not sure we're up to the task."

"Well, they certainly didn't teach us how to do this in school. And yet, there's plenty that we can try, starting with real postmortems that go deeper than the 'Mike was careless' explanation. Before we get there, we have to establish that no one will be fired, demoted, ostracized, or otherwise punished for doing their jobs —for doing what makes sense given the information available at the time. We have to establish that 'accountability' doesn't just mean 'blame.' Being accountable is being beyond blame. Being accountable is accepting responsibility for our actions, and providing the full account, without accepting the blame. So we can learn. And only through this learning can we make our organization more resilient to failures that will inevitably happen. So that we can all make more money."

Raj put his hands behind his head and leaned back in his chair, a hint of a smile on his face. "I get the feeling that you came here to ask me something, not just to share your philosophy of life."

Ollie smiled. "How did you know? What do you think about spending a bit more time investigating the last outage?"

"You mean, yet another postmortem?"

"A real one this time, one with all the groups represented. And including a bit more of your group's P.O.V."

"Man, that's a lot of people. The trial of the century, read all about it!"

"A blameless postmortem, please, so that it doesn't devolve into that."

"And how do you suggest we convince people that this postmortem will be different?"

"First we have to talk to Roger."

12

Paradigm Shift

"You seem preoccupied," Linda said. She was sitting at a small table across from Roger in his office during their weekly check-in meeting. Behind Roger, a large, square window that could not be opened, framed a dreary, darkening sky.

"I'm getting a lot of pressure from the E.C.," he said. "They want assurance that we're not going to have any more trading outages."

"That's not possible," Linda said.

Roger shrugged.

"OK, well, do you have time for a few things related to this?" Linda said.

"All good things, surely," Roger said.

"So, Bill and Ollie and I, we've all been speaking a lot about outages, and what we can do about them. We actually don't know how risky our current situation is."

"Oh, dear lord, what do you mean?"

"We've got a lot of interdependent, interconnected systems. Very complex. It's hard to predict exactly how they might work or fail."

"Don't we have enough experts?"

"We have plenty of experts, but they're not working together much. And they're not focused on the whole system—only their own parts. Like, did you notice how Raj behaved when we talked about the last outage?"

"Nothing unusual. Raj was being Raj."

"He was relieved to not be in the hot seat. We were all relieved to not be Bill that afternoon. We all thought that maybe our teams were different than Bill's, that maybe such things couldn't happen to us. But the problem is that we need Raj's software to work, and Bill's networks, and Ollie's servers. If they don't work, the firm can't trade."

"Yes, yes, I know, none of us succeeds unless we all succeed, and we all fail if one of us fails. But this wasn't about that. I shouldn't have to hold you accountable for a network malfunction. You had nothing to do with that."

"Just to be clear," Linda said, feeling a little tweaked, "When you say 'hold accountable,' do you mean 'job on the line'?"

"All our fucking jobs are on the line!" Roger screamed. "Don't you realize that?"

"I do, Roger," Linda said. "And that's part of the problem."

"What is, exactly, the problem? Is the problem not that some engineer took down the network?"

"That engineer was Mike, and Mike was also the reason we were able to trade for months and even years before. He was part of the reason that we got our bonuses last year. He and people on his team kept the network running. It's not that there weren't issues—there are always issues. But Mike worked around them, or fixed them, before anyone would notice."

"And we are eternally and sincerely grateful that he was doing his job."

"Bill fired the guy who kept the network running for years. What did it take to successfully run a network as large as ours, or to bring it back up after the outage? We've just lost part of that knowledge. And not only that, but when people's jobs are on the line the way they are now, they have an incentive to keep quiet about problems or potential issues instead of sharing what they know. They protect their turf, instead of collaborating. That limits our ability to learn from when things work and when they fail. We lose visibility into our big, complex systems. We could very well be veering into completely uncharted, dangerous territory that would make the previous outage feel tame by comparison. And we might not know it until it's too late."

"So you're suggesting that the way to fix this problem is to get the people who take our networks down off the hook? Maybe even reward them for their good deeds with lifetime employment?"

"Not quite. But you should know that Bill and Ollie are planning to ask you at our staff meeting to no longer fire or punish anyone for causing outages, as long as they provide a full account of what happened."

"You're joking."

"If they can't guarantee this protection for their teams, they're thinking of resigning."

"Thinking?"

"They've almost convinced Raj to do the same."

"And you? What about you?"

"I believe that what we'll learn from people being fully accountable is much more valuable than what we gain by punishing them. It will also boost morale, and help with employee retention. It'll improve the firm's resilience, and ultimately our bottom line. We talk a lot about making the firm a 'learning organization'—well, here's a very concrete step we can take to maximize learning. We want our employees to innovate? Being able to fail in a safe way and learn from it will encourage more innovation. Or we can continue on our current path, and effectively encourage our employees to find innovative ways to limit their personal exposure and liability. Or find employment elsewhere."

Roger stayed silent for a few moments. "You still haven't told me if you're going to resign if I don't agree to support this."

"You know what?" Linda replied. "I've been with the firm for a long time, and I like it here. I want to see the firm succeed. I believe that this can help all of us, including you. And I'm not afraid of leaving."

Linda got up from the chair. "Roger, I wanted to tell you all of this so that you can think it over and be prepared for the staff meeting. It's a paradigm shift, and it does require courage and leadership. But I don't think you got to where you are by cowering in corners."

13

Executive Support

"Is there anything else we need to discuss?" Roger asked, looking around the room. The staff meeting was drawing to a close, and Bill, Ollie, Raj, and Linda had just finished giving brief updates about their past week and sharing their plans for the next. Bill cleared his throat, and spoke more slowly than usual.

"Actually, there is one more thing, Roger. The four of us have been talking a lot about the last outage, and how we dealt with it. We all agree that we could learn more from it."

"Could you?" asked Roger. "I was under the impression that we already identified the root cause."

"We've constructed a comfortable story," Ollie said, "with a simple and single root cause—a villain. And having done that, we short-circuited the possibility for developing any deeper understanding of the complex systems we work with. We haven't really made them safer or more resilient."

"Are you saying that Mike didn't cause the outage?"

"Roger," Bill said, "How was it that Mike was able to do that? What conditions needed to be present for the network to crash? These are the important questions."

"I'm guessing you know the answer to these questions?"

"We know some of the conditions," Bill said. "The security patch, for instance, is one of them. The fact that it was the biggest trading day on record is probably another one. But because we didn't really dig deeply enough, there are most certainly other conditions that we missed."

Bill turned to look at Raj, who shifted uncomfortably in his seat. "For instance," he said, "we didn't look at the application layer. At all."

"Or, for that matter, the system side of things," added Ollie.

"And I'm sure," said Linda, "there were things that the client-services folks know that could be material in reducing the impact of future outages."

"So what would you like to do?" Roger asked, turning to Bill.

"Roger," said Bill, "we need to bring Mike back for another postmortem."

Roger shot Linda a quick look.

"I believe," Bill continued, "that Mike's separation agreement, which he signed when he was let go, has a provision for providing information. I think we've used it before when we had R.I.F.s and needed some information that wasn't documented."

"OK," Roger said, narrowing his eyes. "I'll ask Elaine to have a look at the separation agreement. Assuming we're not exposing the firm to additional liability...." He hesitated for a moment. "Do you think Mike would want to participate? Feels to me like rubbing salt in the wound. Can't we do it without him?"

"I talked to Mike," Bill said. "He's taking it pretty hard, as you can imagine, but I actually think it'll be good for him—maybe even therapeutic—to have his side of the story heard. It won't be comfortable—and not just for Mike. But I definitely think it'll be beneficial for everyone."

"All right then," said Roger. "Let's see what Elaine says. I'm quite interested to see what you might discover. I can't imagine anything drastically different from what we've already gathered, but I'm glad to see that all four of you seem to be in this together. I would love to see more collaboration between you. Assuming we have Elaine's blessing, I'm looking forward to taking part in the event."

"Um," Bill said, "that might not be such a good idea, Roger."

"Pardon?"

"Yeah. So, we all know that we deal rather harshly with folks who make mistakes."

"I'd say that we deal with them rather fairly. We want to show everyone that some mistakes are quite unacceptable."

"It's arguable whether this prevents such mistakes from happening," said Bill, hesitating.

Raj interrupted. "It certainly prevents people from sharing important information—information that can prevent future mistakes. Information that can make our systems more resilient. Information that is more valuable than punishment."

Roger said, "So you think my presence will keep people from fully disclosing such information. Do you all agree on this?"

Bill, Ollie, and Raj said "yes" in unison. Linda nodded.

"Very well, then," said Roger after a brief pause. "Do you think that the same individuals will be forthright with you? After all, it's you who have the power to fire them."

"It won't be easy," said Bill. "The first step—and we're all in agreement on this—is to not punish anyone for sharing what they know. We'll have to emphasize this again and again. We want to guarantee that no one is fired for disclosing what they know. More important, we'll have to actually follow through on that."

"Before we start any postmortem," said Linda, "we'll have to set—or, more accurately, reset—the context, and remind everyone that the point is not to judge, reprimand, or punish, but to understand and learn from what happened. Punishing someone won't change the past. But it certainly will inhibit us from learning about our systems, which will make them more fragile in the future."

"Right, then," Roger concluded after a brief pause. "Honestly, I'm not completely comfortable with any of this this, but I'm willing to see how it goes. You have my support, for now."

14

Complex, Adaptive Systems

Ollie picked up the phone in his office. It was Raj on the other end. "Hey, buddy, are you looking at the email I just sent you?" he asked.

"Not yet," Ollie replied, scanning his inbox for an email from Raj. It was hard to miss, with a subject like "COMPLEXITY!!! SCIENCE!!!" Ollie opened the email and saw a wavy diagram labeled "Cynefin."

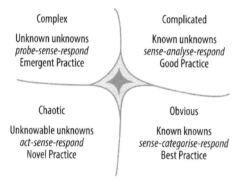

"Dude, I've been researching this complexity stuff that we've been talking about, and I found a *Harvard Business Review* article from 2007 by David Snowden and Mary Boone that introduces this framework called 'Cynefin.' It's a way of thinking about complexity. And this framework is not just philosophy—it's based on complexity science, and it's practical, it's usable."

"Whoa, Raj, slow down. I'm looking at the diagram, but I'm not sure what to make of it yet."

"All right. What we have here, my friend, is a framework that buckets systems into one of the five domains: obvious, complicated, complex, chaotic, and, finally, unknown."

"I see the first four... Where is the unknown one?"

"It's right in the middle. It's also known as 'disorder.'"

"OK, got it. Go on."

"Let's start with obvious systems. Imagine a fast-food chain restaurant. The deep fryer station. There's a very well-understood process of how to make fries reliably. It's documented, and it's highly optimized. There's a best practice, which can be taught and followed by anyone with only a little training. That's how you can get the same fries in any franchise, from Venice, Italy, to Venice, Florida. The process for making fries is highly constrained; the cooks don't get to choose the type of potatoes—they come frozen, precut, and are made from specially grown potatoes. There's even a playbook for when things go wrong: Fries too soggy? See page 39, and turn up the heat by 5 degrees. No room for creativity here, just follow the process."

"This is making me hungry, Raj."

"Buddy, the following will make you even hungrier. Now imagine you're in a fancy, five-star restaurant. You've got a kitchen full of highly experienced chefs, and on this day they, too, are making fries. But this time, the system is a lot less constrained. The chef went to the market that morning and bought some blue potatoes in season, and some organic leeks. She picked up some truffle oil, too, and is now in the kitchen making fancy pommes frites. She's following a basic recipe, but there's a lot more creativity and a lot more experience required. You know what else she's doing that no one at any fast-food restaurant does?"

"Making a living wage?"

"Ha! Yes, and she's also tasting the frites along the way, adding a little salt, or a little more scallions. So in this domain (the complicated-systems one), you still have a recipe to follow—what you might call a 'good practice'—but you need a whole lot more experience in order to operate here, especially when things go wrong. That's why this one is called the 'domain of experts.' Also, complicated systems are far less constrained than obvious ones, but both are still within the realm of ordered domains."

"OK, I'm with you so far."

"Now, my friend, imagine you're watching a cooking competition show. In this particular episode, the 12 participants are given some very loose constraints: ingredients—which feature potatoes—and one hour. Each of the chefs has a lot of freedom to cook whatever and however he or she likes. There are no recipes that they must follow, and they have to improvise a great deal. If we zoom out to look at the entire show kitchen buzzing with activity, we see a dozen parallel experiments going on. Even if this is an elimination challenge, for most of the contestants, these experiments are safe-to-fail experiments. They won't die, even if they get eliminated from the competition. We expect some of the dishes to be mediocre, some of them possibly downright bad, and maybe one or two stand-outs. But no one knows in advance who's going to win, and previous experience is not that valuable here."

"Potato ice cream might just be the best or worst idea in the world."

"You've got the idea about the kinds of things that could come out of these complex, adaptive situations. OK, so now, let's move into the chaotic domain, which, like the complex domain, contains unordered systems. Imagine you've unleashed a gang of toddlers into the same kitchen. No constraints. They're running around with knives, throwing things around, locking one another in freezers, and of course, playing with gas stoves."

"A toddler with a sous-vide machine! What a nightmare!"

Raj laughed. "These chaotic systems are, luckily, very short lived. Someone usually steps in and sets some constraints, moving the system into a more ordered domain."

"'No running with the knives' might be one of the constraints."

"Indeed. In both the complex and the chaotic domains, there's no best practice—not even good practice. We can't predict how things will go in advance, and we might not even be able to establish causality in retrospect. The point is, we have to act differently than we do in the more ordered domains, if we find ourselves working within these unordered ones."

"This is pretty cool, Raj!"

"Yup. So within which domain do you think we most often operate?"

"Certainly not the obvious one, even though there are small armies of consultants that will sell you a 'best practice' for pretty much anything. I'd say we're mostly in the complicated or complex domains. And when we have outages, almost certainly in the complex or chaotic ones."

"Right. Assuming you're working within a complex system is probably a safe default. Most of the time we don't know how our systems are working, and whether the changes we're making will work or backfire. But we can experiment in safe-to-fail ways, and find out more about the constraints of our systems. We can develop heuristics about how to act within them. And, with some luck, we can move these systems into the more predictable and ordered domains by adjusting the constraints. This is something that humans are quite good at."

"This is really fantastic, Raj! Great find. I think it will really help ground all the discussions that we're having about the recent outage."

"I also think it'll help us further convince Roger that we need to change how we deal with outages and the people involved with them. This helps us build credibility."

"Have you sent it to Roger yet?"

"No. But I'll get on his schedule right now."

15

The Learning Review

Whenever Bill was running late, he always asked himself "What am I avoiding?" Today, as he slowly walked down the hall toward the conference room, the answer was unmistakable: although he intuitively felt sure about the new way of dealing with failures and outages—grounded in complexity science and human factors—he also wished he could gently ease into this new world with a little less at stake. Instead, he was headed toward what he knew would be a very difficult conversation, revisiting the biggest outage in recent history. His companions on this journey were also recent converts, inexperienced and unaware of the potential shortcomings of this approach. "Don't try this at home, folks," he thought as he opened the conference room door, and saw Mike seated on one side of the table, and Ollie, Raj, and Linda on the other.

"Glad you could join us," Raj said, flashing a mischievous smile.

Bill sat down next to Ollie. "Sorry I'm late." He cleared his throat. "First of all, Mike, thanks for being here."

Mike nodded.

"We wanted to redo the postmortem of the network outage, and learn more about what happened. We're calling this the 'learning review,' and it's going to be a bit different from the postmortems we've done before."

"Well, for one, you can't fire me," said Mike.

"I'm glad you brought up the elephant in the room," said Linda. "Are you worried that this learning review will turn into another blame session?"

"There's certainly a track record of just that," Mike said.

"It's hard to be open with so much at stake," Linda said.

"Yes. But, look, even without all that, it's not exactly my idea of a fun time to dig through the rubble of outages past, especially ones that I've caused."

"So you don't want to be here?"

"I'm here mostly because Bill asked me to be here. I honestly don't know what I can do or say that I haven't already said or done. I don't know what you're after, exactly."

"So you feel forced into a situation that seems hopeless and pointless?"

Mike paused for a moment. "Yes, that pretty much sums it up."

Linda took a breath. She looked directly at Mike and nodded slightly.

"I just don't like being on trial," he said after a long silence. He exhaled loudly, letting his shoulders relax a bit.

"Believe me," Ollie said, "I don't like being the jury. And look, we're even seated like it's some kind of congressional interrogation." He stood up, and rolled his chair to Mike's side of the table. Linda, Raj, and Bill followed, completing a circle.

Mike looked right and left, with a slight smile. "We gonna sing 'Kumbaya' now?" Everyone laughed. The room felt more relaxed.

Finally, Ollie said, "Mike, thank you again for being here. I know it's not easy. We're trying something new, and I hope you'll humor us."

"How is this learning review different from a postmortem?" Mike asked.

"Fundamentally, in a learning review, we recognize that we're most likely working with a complex system, which requires a different approach than working with other types of systems. We know that in complex systems, the relationship between causes and effects can be teased out only in retrospect, if ever. We're also not looking for a single root cause. Instead, we hope to understand the multitude of conditions, some of which might be outside our control. We also accept that some of the conditions will remain unknown and unknowable.

"Also, so many times in the past, our search for the root cause has led us to the individuals we thought caused the incident. But in the learning-review framework, if we ever get to a single root cause—especially if it's a person—we know we're not digging deep enough."

"And, so we don't take a shortcut to blame," Raj added. "Let's remember that the single root cause of all functioning and malfunctioning systems is impermanence. If you've got to blame something, blame impermanence."

"That's right," said Ollie. "And to make sure that we don't take that shortcut to blame, we treat anything disclosed during a learning review as protected information—meaning it won't be used against the people who share it."

"Where were you when I needed you? That's pretty revolutionary, if it's true," said Mike.

"It is revolutionary for us," said Bill, smiling. "And we've got Roger's support for it. With learning reviews, we're hoping to make our systems more resilient. This requires full accountability, which requires going beyond blame and punishment."

"We also want to learn not just what went wrong," Ollie said, "but what went right—what usually goes right. We're typically overly focused on failures, forgetting that the same systems—including the people working in them—produce both positive and negative outcomes. Mostly positive, in fact—we certainly don't have outages every hour or even every day!"

"And finally," Ollie continued, "we'll be mindful of cognitive biases, which will invariably show up. They're dangerous because they'll make us jump to conclusions too quickly, oversimplify things, and to make incorrect causal attributions. Perhaps the most prominent one is hindsight bias. Biases are pretty hard to spot in oneself, but easier to see in others."

Ollie looked around the circle. "Are we all OK with naming the biases when we see them?" Everyone nodded in agreement. "OK, then, with your permission, I'll be the facilitator. Bill's going to take notes."

Bill got up and walked over to a whiteboard.

"You did always jump at a chance to breathe in marker fumes," Mike said, laughing.

"Well, you know, every little bit helps in our line of work," said Bill, closing his eyes, and taking a long whiff of the uncapped black marker. "All right," he said, still laughing, "let's get started." He quickly drew a timeline on the whiteboard.

16

The Timeline

"So, Mike, take us back," said Ollie, "to the Thursday six weeks ago when you learned about the patch."

"Sure," said Mike. "It was a dark and stormy night, and suddenly my Black-Berry started to vibrate ominously with news of an emergency security patch from our networking vendor. I reviewed the release notes, and it did seem pretty urgent. If left unpatched, an attacker could penetrate our network and view or modify any network traffic. This wasn't in the notes, but I heard through the grapevine that this vulnerability was recently used to steal customer information at the headquarters of Castle-Mart."

"So it seemed reasonable that we would want to apply this patch as soon as possible?"

"Yes. All financial institutions are targets for all kinds of attacks, so we have to take potential security risks seriously."

"How often do you apply security patches like these?"

"Pretty routinely. I'd say there's at least one security patch a quarter, some-times more frequently than that."

"At the same time," said Bill, "you were being quite thorough—you didn't deploy the patch directly to production without testing."

"Objection, your honor!" said Ollie. "That's a counterfactual!"

"Wait, what?" asked Bill. "I thought I was commenting on Mike's thoroughness."

"You were," Ollie replied. "But Mike didn't deploy directly to production. It's not what happened, and therefore a counterfactual."

Bill chuckled. "Man! This is going to be tough. OK, instead of using a coun-terfactual—and thank you for pointing it out, Ollie—I'll say this: Mike, you deployed the patch to our testing environment first."

"Correct," said Mike. "Counterfactual or not, we don't deploy anything without testing it first."

"For a sense of scale," asked Raj, "how often do you make changes?"

"All changes across the network globally?"

"Yes."

"I'd say we make between a few hundred and a few thousand changes to our network each day. Most of the changes are very small. Some are a bit more impactful. Some are automated, and others are done manually."

"Do you try all the changes in the test environment first?"

"No, most of the changes we make are routine. We have tools that validate the changes and catch many errors and issues before they're deployed. But changes deemed especially risky—like the patch in question—these changes are deployed to our test environment, where we then run lots of automated and manual tests. For instance, we simulate network load and see how things hold up."

"How many changes cause outages?"

"Raj, that sounds a lot like linear causality," Bill said. "I'm not sure that applies here, given the complexity of the system."

"Right. I'm trying to estimate how many things go right versus wrong."

"There are also likely errors that we introduce into the environment that don't wind up contributing to outages."

"Sure, we don't have to be exact. Order of magnitude will do."

"In the past year," Mike said, "we've had maybe 10 outages? None of them as severe as the last one. They lasted a few minutes each, at most, and did not always stop the trading."

"Assuming a thousand changes per day, on average," Raj said, "that's close to 400,000 changes in the last year. Kind of surprising that we don't have more failures."

"Maybe that's availability bias in action," said Ollie. "When we do have outages, they're big, memorable, painful events, so we tend to overestimate their likelihood."

"Huh. I've never thought of it that way," said Bill.

Ollie pointed to the whiteboard. "Getting back to the timeline. What kind of testing did we do on the security patch?"

"We did load testing," said Mike. "We generated tons of network traffic to see how the router behaved under load."

"And how did it do?"

"Just fine, no issues. It's worth mentioning that the test environment is a scaled-down version of our production environment. It would be cost prohibitive —and pretty much infeasible—to build an exact replica. And, of course, the network traffic is simulated. Simulated ain't the real thing, and there are things that we can discover only in the real, production environment."

"We've made a very reasonable trade-off," said Ollie. "Instead of building a full-scale replica, we built something much smaller and economical."

"Economical and gets us a .003% change-to-outage ratio," said Raj, showing everyone a fancy calculator app on his tablet. "Can we make it better?"

"Every time there's an issue," Mike answered, "we learn a little more about our system. We can use that knowledge to make the system better, more resilient. For instance, we can write tests for any newly identified conditions of failure."

"Have we done it after the last outage?"

"I haven't," said Mike, looking down. "I wasn't here."

"It's a bit premature to think about remediation," said Ollie. "Bill, can you please note 'testing,' so that we can return to it later? We've got quite a few more things to learn here. Going back to the timeline, it sounds like things were going quite well during the testing, and the patch was eventually applied in production, where it ran without apparent issues for over six weeks."

"Over those weeks, we did experience a steady increase in trading volume," Mike said. "We designed the network to handle several times that volume—or so we thought—and it was performing well. We had a few high utilization alerts, and we investigated a few of them, but found everything working normally."

"So at the time, these alerts didn't seem significant?" Ollie asked.

"There was nothing that seemed out of the ordinary," Mike said. "We get a ton of alerts, most of which we've learned to ignore. They're mostly noise."

"I know we're not supposed to talk about remediation," Bill said, "but the noise in the monitoring or alerting system seems significant. I'm going to make a note of this in the remediation 'parking lot,' so we can return to it later."

"Good call, Bill," said Ollie. "Let's return to the fateful Tuesday. Mike, when did you first get an indication that things might not be going well?"

"We started to get high-utilization alerts at around 11 a.m. I didn't think much... What I mean is, I thought, based on previous alerts that didn't correlate to any noticeable performance degradation, that these alerts were probably nothing. But they kept coming, and the utilization kept climbing from 70 to 80 percent. When it reached 85 percent, I decided to check things out. I logged into the router, and issued a status command. All of a sudden, I got disconnected from the router."

"What were you thinking at this time?"

"I thought, 'This is odd.' I tried to reconnect to the router, but it seemed to be down. I got a notification on my BlackBerry that the standby router had taken over, which is what's supposed to happen. I checked the monitoring system, and traffic seemed to be moving; in fact, the utilization was down a bit into the 70 percent range. I was feeling pretty good, actually. I was a little concerned about what happened to the primary router—it didn't feel right the way that it went down—but since things were working again, I thought we could investigate that later. I had no idea that I had just turned onto a one-way street and was speeding the wrong way with no brakes."

Mike took a deep breath, and shook his head.

"No one had any idea, Mike," Raj said. "And what we also didn't know at the time is that a week and a half prior, my team updated a configuration setting on our main equities-trading platform. It was the time-out setting, which specifies how long the system should wait in case it gets disconnected before trying to reconnect. The engineer who made the change thought the setting was measured in minutes. Turns out, it was measured in seconds, and he set the system to retry every second in case of connectivity issues."

"When did we figure this out?" asked Linda.

"Last Friday," Raj replied. "The engineer panicked, changed back the time-out setting right after the outage. He even modified the change log so that no one would find out."

"He must have been terrified!" said Linda. "How did you manage to find out?"

"We ran our own little learning review, and he came forward. Provided a full account."

"Amazing," Mike said. "So that explains the sudden surge in traffic after the primary router failed. I've been wondering why the utilization surged to 90 percent a few minutes after the failover—it didn't seem that the increased market volume could be causing that much of a spike. In any case, that's when I logged into the standby router, and all hell broke loose. Well, it did, right after I used the same status command, which bricked the primary router."

Mike crossed his arms. "I'm still having trouble with this," he said, shaking his head. "I really should have known better. I should have been more careful not to repeat the same mistake twice."

"Your honor..." Bill started.

Mike cut him off, "I know, I know. Counterfactuals, hindsight, and all that. But knowing that doesn't make me feel better. I really expect more from myself."

Linda looked at Mike and said, "You wished your experience would have tipped you off that you were in drastically different territory?"

"The thing is, even after I took down the second router with the same damn status command, I still didn't think I was doing anything wrong."

The room was silent. The phone conferencing system was quietly buzzing because of radio interference from a nearby mobile phone. Bill popped the cap back onto the marker, and placed it on the whiteboard. Linda nodded slightly at Mike.

"I guess I needed to say that," he said.

"We hear you, Mike," said Linda.

Mike leaned back in his chair, letting his hands fall on his knees. "When I play back that moment," he continued, "and think about what I knew at that time, I can't come up with another set of actions that would make sense. In fact, it took a while before I understood that we'd drifted into a totally new world, where the most innocuous, routine command—one that we all use hundreds if not thousands of times a day—would crash the router."

Raj cleared this throat. "From the perspective of complexity science, we're either in the chaotic or the complex domains. In either case, the relationship between cause and effect cannot be established in real time. Experience is not useful here. If we're in the chaotic domain, the right thing to do is just to act—to do something and see what happens. If we're in a complex domain, we probe— try a few things that might possibly work. Either way, your actions were reasonable, coherent, and appropriate. Fundamentally, they helped us learn that the system had drifted, as you said, into a state that we label 'failure,' but, of course, is just a different state of a working system."

"So how did we get out of this state?" asked Ollie.

"We called the router vendor," Mike replied, "and eventually got a senior engineer on the line. Within a half hour of that, we decided to roll back the patch —meaning, get the router to a previous version of the software. We didn't know if that would fix the issue, but it seemed like it might work. So we did that around 1:20 p.m. But now there was so much network traffic that the utilization immediately spiked to a hundred percent. Things were flowing incredibly slowly, but at least the router wasn't crashing anymore.

"Now we had to manually disconnect parts of the network in order to reduce traffic and stabilize the network. This proved tricky and time-consuming because we designed the network to be resilient, and route around failures. So when we would disable a network path, the traffic would start flowing through another route. Talk about unintended consequences. It took us roughly five hours to work through this. Unfortunately, we finished after the market closed, and that left a bunch of unwanted positions on our books that we couldn't unwind until the following day. Which is why the firm lost money on some of them."

The room fell quiet again. Ollie tapped his finger on the table. "Did we cover most of it?"

"We covered most of the technical timeline," said Linda. "Before we go on, I want to add some color from a client-services perspective. As you can imagine, we started to get a lot of calls from our clients—both internal and external. We even got calls from the press! We were, frankly, overwhelmed by the volume. Even more important, we didn't know what was going on until about 1:08 p.m., when the crisis management group call was finally started."

"Mike called me at 12:45 p.m.," said Bill, "while I was at lunch. It took a while to find the crisis management folks and for them to start the call."

"That sounds like another potential area to look into," said Bill, adding Crisis Management to the Remediation list on the whiteboard, which, by that point, also contained Testing, Alert Noise, Internal and External Communication, and Client-Services Call Volume. "Is now the right time to talk about remediation items—things we might do differently in the future?"

"Well, if no one has anything to add to the timeline," Ollie answered, "it probably is. But let's take a short break, shall we?"

"Amen!" said Mike, smiling broadly.

17

The Town Hall

The auditorium was at full capacity. It could barely contain the entire New York I.T. group, and engineers from remote locations joined via videoconference. On the raised stage at the front of the room, Roger was seated at the table covered with the blue tablecloth. Raj and Ollie sat on his left side, Bill and Linda on his right. There was an echoing ping sound and buzzing across the room—the calendars on the computers and smartphones reminding those in attendance that the meeting was starting. Ever punctual, Roger cleared his throat, and moved the microphone closer.

"Welcome, everyone. Thank you for taking the time out of your busy day to be here. I'd like to talk about the outage that happened a few weeks ago."

Roger paused, noting the tension in the room. He took a deep breath. "I, like many of you, thought that we had dealt with the last outage," he said. Unfortunately, upon further reflection, we see that we've learned very little from this incident. Our ability to learn from our mistakes—our ability to adapt—is clearly paramount to the firm's success.

"Over the years, we've drifted toward a culture of blame, detrimental to our ability to learn. To be quite blunt, if anyone made a mistake or was part of an accident, we blamed them for it. We reprimanded, demoted, or worse, discarded people. Sadly, this approach has not made our systems more resilient to failures —quite the contrary, as evidenced by the recent outages, which were unprecedented in both their duration and cost.

"With the perfect vision afforded by hindsight, we can spend a lot of time ruminating on what we could or should have done. That is counterproductive; the past is past. We need to acknowledge and learn from our mistakes, and move forward, focusing instead on what we will do now and in the future.

"First of all, and perhaps most importantly, starting now we will guarantee that no one providing a full account of their actions during incidents will be penalized in any way. The information that you provide during postmortems cannot and will not be used against you—not as a reason for demotion, or reduced compensation, or any other disciplinary action.

"I imagine that some of you aren't entirely convinced. I understand completely—this is a rather radical departure. And yet it's not as radical as it seems. Take, for example, the U.S. Forest Service, which protects its employees from federal prosecution for any information that they provide as part of a postmortem, or, as they call it, "learning review." Mind you, these are incidents that, unlike ours, sometimes result in loss of life in forest fires.

"This is going to take some work. It's going to require a readjustment. I am personally committed to seeing this take root here at the firm. If you feel that you have been, or are being, punished in any way in connection with your part in an outage, please come to me.

"We work with some of the brightest, most dedicated technologists on Wall Street. I firmly believe that when we utilize our collective ability to learn and adapt, we will build the most successful financial institution in the world.

"Now I must thank several people for bringing this to my attention—namely Raj, Ollie, Bill, and Linda. We've been having extensive discussions on this topic over the last several weeks, and they've developed an amazing depth of knowledge and insight into how we can improve in this area. They will be involved in all serious-incident reviews going forward, and we will be sharing the results of our learning with everyone in I.T. and beyond. They've also put together a framework for conducting learning reviews that everyone can use. I realize that this is a lot to process. What are your questions?"

Roger scanned the room, which was silent. He searched the room for a young project manager named Ami, who had a knack for asking what everyone was thinking. He found him toward the back of the room, leaning on a wall. Ami was wearing his usual grey three-piece suit, a pink shirt, and no tie. His hair was tightly cropped, goatee neatly trimmed.

"Ami, you usually have questions," Roger said. The room erupted with laughter.

Ami stood up, red in the face, and projecting his voice loudly, said, "As a matter a fact, I do have a question. First, I'd like to say that I think this is great, and I'm looking forward to learning how to do postmortems better, without a fear of blame or punishment hanging over our heads. The question I have is, what about Mike?"

There was a rustling as everyone in the room turned their attention back to Roger.

"What a fantastic question, Ami!" Roger said. "I spoke to Mike earlier this week, and apologized for the way we treated him. In retrospect, we made a huge mistake, and lost a great engineer. We've offered him his job back. Unfortunately for us, he's been picked up by another bank. I can't blame him."

The last sentence got a few chuckles from the crowd, and several more hands went up.

"Anthony." Roger was speaking to an engineer in the front row.

"What does this learning-review framework look like?" asked Anthony.

Roger turned to Ollie. "Do you want to take this one?"

"Absolutely," said Ollie.

18

The Learning Review Framework

1. Set the context.

- The purpose of the learning review is to learn so that we can improve our systems and organizations. No one will be blamed, shamed, demoted, fired, or punished in any way for providing a full account of what happened. Going beyond blame and punishment is the only way to gather full accounts of what happened—to fully hold people accountable.

- We're likely working within complex, adaptive systems, and thus cannot apply the simplistic, linear, cause-and-effect models to investigating trouble within such systems. (See *A Leader's Framework for Decision Making* by David J. Snowden and Mary E. Boone.)

- Failure is a normal part of the functioning of complex systems. All systems fail—it's just a matter of time. (See *How Complex Systems Fail* by Richard I. Cook, MD.)

- We seek not only to understand the few things that go wrong, but also the many things that go right, in order to make our systems more resilient. (See *From Safety-I to Safety-II: A White Paper* by Erik Hollnagel, et al.)

- The root cause for *both* the functioning and malfunctions in all complex systems is impermanence (i.e., the fact that all systems are changeable by nature). Knowing the root cause, we no longer seek it, and instead look for the many conditions that allowed a particular situation to manifest. We accept that not all conditions are knowable or fixable.

— Human error is a symptom—never the cause—of trouble deeper within the system (e.g., the organization). We accept that no person wants to do a bad job, and we reject the "few bad apples" theory. We seek to understand why it made sense for people to do what they did, given the information they had at the time. (From *The Field Guide to Understanding Human Error* by Sidney Dekker.)

— While conducting the learning review, we will fall under the influence of cognitive biases. The most common ones are hindsight, outcome, and availability biases; and fundamental attribution error. We may not notice that we're under the influence, so we request help from participants in becoming aware of biases during the review. (Read *Thinking, Fast and Slow* by Daniel Kahneman.)

2. Build a timeline.

— We want to understand what happened from the perspective of the individuals involved: what did they know, when, and how did it make sense?

— Describe what happened; don't explain.

— The more diverse points of view that you can collect, the fuller the picture of the incident. Encourage and note divergent and dissenting opinions.

— As the facilitator, your job is to listen to discover and verify by synthesizing.

3. Determine and prioritize remediation items, if any. This can be done separately from building a timeline.

4. Publish the learning review write-up as widely as possible.

    If the incident negatively impacted people, consider using the Three Rs ("Regret, Reason, Remedy," from *Drop the Pink Elephant* by Bill McFarlan) to structure the write-up.

During the learning review, listen for, and help participants be aware of blaming, cognitive biases, and counterfactuals ("We could have/we should have/if only we/we didn't"). Use empathy and humor throughout the learning review to defuse tense situations, especially at the beginning. Ask lots of questions, including these:

- Did we know this at the time or is it obvious only in hindsight?

- When did we learn this fact?

- How does knowing the outcome affect our perception of the situation (or the people involved in the incident)?

- Is this a likely explanation because we've recently had a similar problem? How is this situation different?

- Can you please describe what happened without explaining (too much)?

- Any one of us would have done what Bob or Sue did. Let's focus on how it made sense at the time, and what we can do better in the future.

- This sounds like a counterfactual. What actually happened, what did we know, and how did it make sense at the time?

- How do we know this?

Index

A

accountability
  blame vs., 17-18
  corporate definition of, 11
  extending beyond blame, 38
  improper application of, 5
  punishment vs., 43
  rewards vs., 19
  true meaning of, 35
  with learning reviews, 55
adaptation, 21
adaptive system, 34
attribution error, fundamental, 30
automobile analogies (see car, as complex system)
availability bias, 58
Awesome Postmortems workshops, xi

B

bad apples, 13-15
best practice, 50
biases, cognitive, 28-31, 68
black swan event, 34
blame
  accountability vs., 17-18
  and learning reviews, 69
  as barrier to improvement, 38
  as barrier to learning, 63
  downside of, 37-39
  impermanence as, 54
  importance of going beyond, xi
  in complex systems, 13-15
  math homework example, 23

  risks inherent in, 34
  two sides of, 35
Boone, Mary, 49
Buddha, 20
butterfly effect, 21

C

car accident analogy, 14
car key analogy, 13
car, as complex system, 13
change, in complex systems, 19
chaotic system, 34, 51, 61
cognitive biases, 28-31, 55, 68
complex systems, 34, 61
  adaptation in, 21
  barriers to understanding, xi
  change in, 19
  diagnosing problems in, 13-15
  failure in, 19
complex, adaptive systems, 34, 49-52, 67
complexity science, 61
complicated systems, 50
compounded phenomena, 20
context, learning review, 67
counterfactuals, 29, 57, 69
Cynefin, 49

D

distracted driver analogy, 14
domain of experts, 50
drunk driver analogy, 14

About the Author

Dave Zwieback has been working with complex, mission-critical IT systems and teams for two decades. His career spans small high-tech startups, non-profits, and behemoth engineering, financial services, and pharmaceutical firms.

To learn more about Dave, the Awesome Postmortems workshop, and other services offered by his firm, Mindweather LLC, please visit *mindweather.com* or follow @mindweather on Twitter.

Colophon

The cover image is by Jimmy Brown via Flickr. The cover fonts are URW Typewriter and Guardian Sans. The text font is Adobe Minion Pro; the heading font is Adobe Myriad Condensed; and the code font is Dalton Maag's Ubuntu Mono.